T0107416

LIVE TO LIVE

ENCOUNTER HIM

LILOUITEE JOYCE BACCHUS

WestBow Press books may be ordered through
booksellers or by contacting:

WestBow Press
A Division of Thomas Nelson & Zondervan
1663 Liberty Drive
Bloomington, IN 47403
www.westbowpress.com
844-714-3454

ISBN: 979-8-3850-0614-4 (sc)
ISBN: 979-8-3850-0615-1 (e)

Print information available on the last page.

WestBow Press rev. date: 09/13/2023

CONTENTS

PREFACE

It started as a reflection and a thought, an admiration for the wonders of creation and the One who did it all. I was not deeply committed in a way, much less spirit-filled or religious, to say the least. But I was only the instrument with a pen, crafting words as if I were copying.

Therefore, I proclaim that the true author of these writings is none other than the Holy Spirit. Even though back in 1990, during those early days, I was unaware of the gift that was born into my spirit. I remember thinking to myself, "Wow, I am writing poems!" It was a newfound interest that I had never possessed before. I had never delved into poetry, and I was astonished at how the words seamlessly flowed, one line after another, like an unending river.

But as swiftly as this passion arrived, it departed just as fast. In the later part of 1990, I abruptly closed the book on this endeavor, and for thirty long years, it remained out of sight. It seemed, as though these poems were consigned to the archives, or worse, as if they had never existed at all. I never shared them with anyone, never read them aloud to another soul. They remained hidden, waiting patiently to be discovered.

In the year 2019, I found myself immersed in moments of meditation, prayer, and deep reflection on God's boundless mercy and kindness, not only in my own life but in the lives of those around me. The landscape of everyday existence had undergone numerous dramatic transformations, and my personal journey was no exception. At times, it felt like chaos consumed me, but even amidst the storms, the hand of God remained ever-present, faithfully watching over myself and my family. His timing was impeccable, always stepping in when we faltered.

And so, it was during this significant period in 2019 that my profound contemplation and gratitude for His unending goodness, caused the dormant fire within me to be suddenly rekindled.

I was struck with awe and wonderment as these writings took on a new dimension. They were no longer mere poems, but profound messages of admonition, encouragement, warnings, and divine guidance. I found it increasingly difficult to simply categorize them and set them aside in some forgotten archives. They held within them a power and significance that demanded to be shared.

So, as I embarked on writing the first piece in this series, I summoned the courage to pray, "Holy Spirit, grant me the strength to share these words in church on Father's Day." And miraculously, He answered that prayer. The poem titled "My Father" was just the beginning, followed by over two dozen more in rapid succession. The urge to transcribe them by hand and share them with anyone who might benefit from their messages of encouragement and enlightenment grew stronger within me.

Yet, the Lord had even greater plans in store. He provided the essential tools and resources that allowed these writings to reach far beyond my immediate reach. I am truly astonished and filled with gratitude for the way He orchestrates and redirects the paths of humanity. Through these divine words, His love, His redemptive plans, and His profound wisdom are revealed. It is a testament to His grace and mercy, and I am humbled to be a vessel through which His message can be conveyed.

Lilouitee Joyce Bacchus

ACKNOWLEDGEMENT

First and foremost, I acknowledge the inspiration and presence of the Holy Spirit from the inception, who diligently placed the words in my heart, and formulated them in such a way that makes me to know His deep ways and thoughts. To Him let the honor be. Secondly its, my greatest pleasure to acknowledge the zeal and determination of a humble and sincere friend in the Lord Jesus, Marie-France, who propelled me into getting this “work of the Lord done”.

I would like to express my immense gratitude towards Apostle Powell, who was approached by Marie-France and graciously agreed to assist in this endeavor. I am deeply appreciative of his support. Apostle J. Powell, the author of “Seven Keys to Reset Your Mind-Set,” is dedicated to helping new authors write and share their stories as legacies for future generations.

I would like to express my heartfelt gratitude and honor to Pastor Jerome Thomas, my spiritual father in Christ, for his words of encouragement. I also want to extend my thanks and love to my parents, Elizabeth and Charles, who provided me with the best education and unwavering support. I am truly grateful. I cannot forget to acknowledge the incredible support and attentive listening of my husband, Ishmael, and our son, Ishmael Jr., as I shared these inspirational pieces with them. I am confident that my words have somehow impacted them. May all the glory be given to God alone.

GREATEST TREASURE

The universe is vast
Your hand stretches from end to end
Who can fathom the depths and widths?
We are but specks in your eyes
Yet you deem us above all else.

The world is round, and you are at the center
Like a magnet drawing all men to you.
The foundation on which we exist.
What intelligence can man possess.
To understand its metrics.
Limited is he. His very breath depends on you.
His thoughts are consumed in vanity
His efforts are temporal.
Works of worthlessness cling to his fingers.
But you oh Lord, is his treasure.

Visible or invisible, can easily be found.
The vision is clear, and the path illuminated,
By your endless glory and wisdom unfolding
day by day.

I KNOW

I know you care for this.
One worthless sinner far removed.
But now under your wings of grace and love I live.

I know you watch each, and every step I take.
Moving off track against your will.
But still you care.
For you intentionally changed the path, so I know you care.

So many blessings I cannot contain.
For you are always just in time.
Against all odds. You let me know how much you care.

For I can see the evils all around.
But I am in a safe impermeable place.
This time, all the time.
For with a blow from your breath.
And a word from your mouth.
They dissipate beyond their will.
Then I see it's not by chance.

I know from where I came
From the lane of doom and gloom.
And yes, you care, enough to give
me time to turn, to repent.
To change my ways.
Unconditional love.
That's who you are!!

MY EARTHLY VOYAGE

This I remember, I danced over water
And skipped over pools.
But did not fall, your steady arms held me fast.

I gazed into the unknown
The dark hideous ways
You were my eyes and guided me.
As I crossed from tunnel to tunnel
Lest I lost the way.
Along the path was beautiful
The rainbow above, a canopy of colors.
The perfume of sweet, smelling roses
Beads of raindrops sprinkled their petals
Makes it all nature's beauty.

So, once I thought as a child.
And reasoned with no knowledge
But now you prune this tree,
To blossom and to bear
And yield much fruits of wisdom.
So, as I take my steps of decision I still,
Will not lose the way!!

MY FATHER

His name is above all other names
His power is matchless
In heaven and on earth.
His life a legacy of humility and righteousness.
Standing in truth and obedience.

His love un-dimensional.
Agape love, as we understand.
Limitless, fearless, and persevering.
His fight for us, was predestined.
A winner of souls, for me and for you

A friend of sinners
Who ate and drank with them.
Talked and walked with them.
So tireless was His care and compassion,
you cannot imagine!!

His sacrifice was His ultimate goal,
As a father stands in the gap.
To save and protect
So it was, will always be,
As He stood in place of us.
Paid the price of love with His life

Then I reflected, as I stood in Awe

Who is He?

The only One, true, Living God, Jehovah

Our heavenly Father.

Awaiting, with outstretched arms for you and for me.

HOPELESSNESS IS VANITY

Metal is the car
Crumbled together, there's no shape or design
House is the wood, burnt - like
charcoal into ashes, or concrete crushed into dust.
Money is the source, that provides an access to survive.
But unwisely used is more destruction and pain, than gain.

Wealth, fame, and status, sounds good, looks good.
All to be desired. But what is the reward thereof?
If these replace the One,
Who sits on the throne,
Then all is vanity.
RETRACT, RETHINK,
REFRAIN AND REPENT

And confirm your ways,
To the true elements of life
Which cannot be bought, sold, or destroyed.

Is this the promise of the Father?
Yes, indeed, seek first the things of above
Be not a fool to live contrary.
But open the doors to your heart, as He knocks.
For then He will come in and dine with thee.

HE IS PRESENT

Beyond the clear blue skies
Above the green mountain tops
I see and feel the glory of the Lord
I know He is there, every day, every minute.
With eyes fixed on each and everyone.

I wonder at His majesty
I know we cannot measure
Yet, we little stop to think of Him
His mighty works and deed
Done every minute of the day.

The tranquil lake lies right ahead
The scattered buildings at its edge.
Behind the rising parched and green mountains.
Then again, the clear blue heavens.
And I wonder- yes Lord, you are around.

Then I think of all around me.
I care not, for their color, their look, or position.
I care not of my own
But there is one care in my heart,
Our hearts.
Will they be the same as that of Jesus?
In color and contriteness.

THE DAY OF THE LORD

Rejoice! All you heaven and earth.
Sing praises to His Holy name
On bended knees and outstretched arms
The Lord of Lords will soon approach

The book of life which He possess
And then, descends to proclaim.
This great and notable day foretold
So many centuries before.

Rise you servants of the Lord
Let go your trouble and possession
Go gather all His people in.
The harvest time is at hand.

Behold the day is here
Gather nothing for thyself
No shoe, nor bag, or coat, nor hat
For He is all, and in all
For all eternity.

SPRINGS OF JOY

Beyond the rivers of tears
Are springs of joy and peace
Beyond the dark and gloomy paths
Are paths alight by His glory
And beyond life's despair
Is the blessed and eternal hope.

These rivers of tears, are
No wider, longer, or deeper
Than the springs of joy.
And so is the glorious path.
There is no other like it,
Still, we remain in life's despair.

Will you continue along the banks of the river?
Or on the paths of darkness?
Will you see no hope or not know,
His promise of eternal love?
Will you honestly retreat into life's despair?
I pray you will join your hands
And heart, together with His
And be renewed.
In the spirit of the Lord.

A CALL FROM HEAVEN

There is a road up yonder
A road where He trod,
With dusty and with tired feet.
He trod the path of men.

There is a shore
That faces the placid ocean
Where He taught them of His ways
But there was that lonely soul
Who believed wholeheartedly.
And Jesus knew him from the start
And said to Him- "Come"

He looked him straight into the eyes.
At last, his bones were loosed.
As he decided to follow Him
Who trod the paths of men.

Indeed, far away on a hill up yonder
He prayed for you and for me
Again, He is praying and waiting.
He is calling to you and to me - "Come."
My brother, my sister, my friend.
Behold the call of the Father.
Through the working of His Holy spirit.

HE TOUCHED ME

I was asleep. When He touched me
I opened my eyes,
And beheld His magnificence.
And knew it's a whole new world,
Hidden before with glamour and pride,
With hatred and greed.

He touched me on the eyes,
And again, the scales, He removed.
I saw ahead, a whole new kingdom,
A new generation
A people washed in His precious blood.

And I said Lord, why have you touched my eyes?
And He replied, "that you may see",
"Go forth and touch my people".
Again, He touched me,
But this time in my heart.

HIS NAME

I knew Him not, only by name
I saw Him not, for I was blind
I felt Him not, as I was dead
But only knew a name called Jesus.

How very far away I was
A place where many know today
My faith seemed hopeless
Was barren and empty.
For I only knew a name called Jesus.

Then one day as I stumbled
I hit my feet real hard and fell
The path was tough, with rocks and thorns
A path of real destruction.

Then I recalled that name I knew.
Jesus! Jesus! Save my soul.
Only then I realized,
It was not just a name.
It was and is the name of my Father,
My Savior and my Lord.
"Come to my abode and rest you gently".
This day you'll call me
Lord forever.

BE STILL

Sit still and listen to His voice
Be calm, and patient as He speaks.
His voice is calm with tender words.
It tells us of how much He cares.

He is our silent listener
Our need for every hour
Each passing moment we're not alone
He sees our sorrows and shares our joy.

But only we must listen
And learn to give Him honor.
In songs of love and praises of joy.
With steadfast minds and silent prayers.

And we will know that He does care.
For in the midst of desolation,
There is a peace, and a glory,
That shines beyond our tears.
A song within our hearts.

THE HARVEST IS READY

Truly the harvest is ripe.
You see the seasons,
You understand well,
When the fruits are ripe,
For you gather before the spoils.

Truly you understand
Sowing and reaping.
For your kingdom is rich.
Because you work and do not sleep.
And hire laborers in your fields.

It's the same in my kingdom.
The harvest is beyond ripe.
With no one to reap.
Heap of fruits with no laborers.
Lots of wastage,
Lots of spoils.

Will you come and gather for me?
Will you be that faithful servant?
That my kingdom can be enlarged.
My servants are asleep.

They do little, and expect much,
They follow other pathways
And are misled.
When its summer they say
We are in spring.
They misinterpret the times.
And lean on their own understanding.
They flee from my wisdom.
And so, my fruits are going to the spoil.

Today if you hear my voice
Come forth.
Be the laborer in my fields.
Count not the cost.
For I am the wage payer.

You see a dying brother,
A hungry slave,
An abandoned child,
A homeless beggar,
A sinner in need of my word.
This is my harvest.
Go out and reap these souls.
Do not sleep and slumber,
For the harvest is ripe.

HIS AMAZING GRACE

Clear my path Lord, let my trust be,
Beyond the unfolding horizons.
Let my faith surmount,
Higher than the eagles.
Let my love expand daily,
To engulf the lonely downtrodden hearts.
Let my giving be, as the widow's mite, all I can do.
Let my forgiveness, be as you say.
Not counted on my fingers.
For you Lord is limitless.
And I need to follow in your steps.

But as I drop short daily
And did not reach the line as I should.
Your mercy,
Your grace,
And your love,
I will cling to.
For you have no boundaries.

More and more,
I am driven to believe and know,
There is little I can do,
To get into your kingdom.
Our righteousness stands unclean, before you.
Our entry is by your grace only.

The truth is Lord,
Accepting your finished
Work on the cross.
Being obedient to the call.
Never losing sight of you,
Is the most I can pursue.
To run this race, set forth,
By you.

NEW LIFE

I followed Him in the crowd.
I was close behind,
And saw Him on the move.
The blind saw, the deaf heard.
The paralyzed rose up, from the ashes
And the dumb spoke.

It was an intense immense moment.
As the Lord took Him by the hand,
We came to realize,
He is the God, most high.
To be touched by Him,
Is to be touched by the ever glowing,
Light of glory.

Dimness vanishes.
Hopelessness relinquishes.
Failures crumble,
And death flee.

Life springs up,
Like a green, tender shoot.
Living anew, sustained
By His touch.

EMMANUEL, GOD IS WITH US

Rejoice! all you nations,
With shouts of praises,
And let us kneel in adoration.
For a king is born.
The King of Kings,
Emmanuel, God is with us.

All creation stood still.
As angels ushered in His birth.
The shepherds were afraid, but amazed.
For never before a King would be born in a manger.
Directed by a star, born of a virgin whom He created.

Who can believe,
Who can accept the impossible act of God.
Neither scholars, teachers nor theologians.
Neither Jew nor Greek, great, or small.
It was never seen before.
Will not be seen again.

Let us, therefore, offer our gifts,
Gold, frankincense, and myrrh.
We have not.
What then can we offer our King?

Look not under the tree.
Or on the tabletop.
It's not found in tinsels or lights.
Or on the sleigh drawn down
The snowy slopes.
For these will fade away.
But bring Him our gifts
Of love and adoration,
Of goodness, mercy, and forgiveness
Of obedience and repentance,
Goodwill and peace among all men.
For these gifts He will accept.
And these gifts He will treasure,
For they will never fade away.

STAR OF BETHLEHEM

This night was different.
This star was brighter.
Something extraordinary was happening.

The wise men knew it,
And received its message.
From distant lands they travelled,
Over the hills and over the plains.
They travelled in search
Of Christ the King.

On camel backs they rode.
As many days turned into months.
They crossed deserted deserts.
And followed the star, wherever it went.

Great was their expectations.
And tedious their journey.
But joy filled their hearts.
Then suddenly,
The star stood still over a stable.
Where cattle slept,
And lambs' meander.

Could this be the place,
Where the child was born?
It's not a palace or a house.
It seems unreal. Yet with no questioning
Or further debate,
They did dismount their noble ride.
And hurried in to worship the King.
Yes gold, frankincense, and myrrh.
They presented.
All symbols of His kingly life
In silent reverence they stood.
Bewildered at the babe on hay.
Full of joy, peace, and wisdom.
Their journey was over.

Inspired by God, they left.
Returning unnoticed,
Concealing their encounter.
For in their hearts, they knew it.
He was the redeemer
Savior of the world.
Emmanuel, God is with us.

PURSUE THE TRUTH

So, you recognize you are alive,
As you wake.
And that in your state of sleep
You were out
And you recognize when you open your eyes
It took no effort on your side.
And you know for a fact,
It's Him who woke you.
If not, you sleep.

So, let's reason together.
If He gives us life
Being our creator, Elohim is His name.
He is the Way, Light of our path.
He is our good shepherd, Jehovah Rohi.

Leading us all the way.
Jehovah Shalom; Our God of peace.
Jehovah Rapha; Our healer.
Then clearly, He is the most important One to pursue.
Not Peter, John, or Mary.
For they too need Him.

So, then we come to understand,
This one, merciful, loving,
Irreplaceable, Sovereign God,

Is not to be taken, as we please,
But to be honored,
Obeyed and magnified,

For who He is.
So, what takes us this long?
To obey and accept His love
For our souls?
Why do we procrastinate?
Why do we hide our faces?
And live as the heathens do?
Carried to and fro,
Out and about.

What takes us this long?
To accept the only Son of God.
Jesus, our Savior.
Our breath of life
The one who cannot fail
Untouchable by evil and death.

For if we lose Him,
We have lost everything!!

REACH FOR THE PRIZE

I am walking up this hill of glory.
My steps are sure, my mind is made.
As my eyes grow dim,
And my hair turns white.

I am treading up this hill to glory.
My path is clear, but still, I can stumble.
So, I have determined to rise up and continue.

Many are the afflictions.
Many thorns and thistles line the path.
Many sidetracks and distractions.
Scorpions and lions lie in wait.
But I am going to the land of glory.

His perfect love cast out all fear.
For broad is the way to destruction
and narrow the path to freedom.
His abiding presence is all I need.

For my frail heart will let me down,
And my efforts will be in vain.
So, I count on His unfailing grace.
And I count on our bonds of love.
And I count on all His promises.
And these add strength and courage.
To see me through to the hill up yonder.

Then one day I will reach the highest peak.
My track I will see no more.
For what lies ahead
I will stand in awe
At the prize, I was aiming for.

His glory all around
With precious gems
And streets of gold
Transparent walls
Never hidden from His eyes.

Yes, I will drop to my knees.
With all His love,
My destiny is fulfilled.
And forever, I will dwell,
In the house of the Lord.

OUR EARTHLY FATHERS

In His image you are made.
A blueprint of the Master's touch.
Predestined to walk in His steps,
For you possess wisdom, strength,
Intelligence and authority
And hold the keys for directions.

To lead a nation, overlook its borders.
To stand as a shield of protection
for the weak and downtrodden.

Your expertise does not go unnoticed
For you are multipurpose, multitasks.
In the skies, in the fields
On the seas, you venture.

Magnificent castles and mansions,
are built by your skillful hands.
The world is beautified, by your touch.
Creative arts depict your talents.

You may not fully understand,
For your responsibility goes far and beyond.
A covering, a shield, a role model,
a high priest for the Lord.
You are truly blessed, you are loved.
You are unique. So, stand tall looking up,
To the One, who cares for you.
Abba Father.

THE TRUMPET WILL SOUND

Now is the time, now is the day.
Do not hide or put your light under a bushel.
Stand out from the rest and cast your cares
into the seas, give them to Him.

For the trumpet will sound.
When? We do not know.
But sufficient to know is, He knows.
And His spirit is roaming the earth.
Gird up your loins
And gather up the remnants.
Prepare your soul,
For the anchor will hold
So, faint not and gather not the spoils.

Even at the door, is the sound of His steps.
Can you hear His gentle whisper?
Then open, open the doors, they are closed!!

Who can believe and who will listen?
Wake up, wake up, and slumber not.
Eat your grain in haste, giving thanks and praise.
Praying unceasingly for who will have faith.
And who will have a pure heart.
Who will He find in truth and love,

With flames of fire, His chariots are set,
So, listen, wait, endure, and pray.
For suddenly, in the twinkling of an eye
The trumpet will sound.

THE REASON

Did you hear? Did you understand?
Or did someone tell you?
Maybe you read it. That the Lord of the universe,
And heavens came here.
In human form he presented himself.

Did you give it a thought?
The purpose of His human presentation?
For no one can touch God.
He came to retrieve the lost, the stolen,
The downtrodden and castaway souls.

This was His "soul" intention.
Light came to destroy the evil agenda.
But today we can see man's persistence, as he chose
To embrace darkness and shun the Light.

Do you know His heart is grieving?
As His eyes pierce, every corner of the earth,
Sorrow fills His heart.
Yes, He is longsuffering and patient,
His grace abounds. He chose to wait for you.
Do you understand? That time is closer and closer,
Like a vapor is lost, to wake into a new day.
Is one of the greatest gifts, He gives.

Oh, lonely soul!
Why do you let it go, for tomorrow is a chance,
you cannot count.

Know the truth, surrender to His love,
His magnificent power.
Then you will understand,
Only then you will know,
Why He descended to earth.

MASTER OF ALL

We are nothing without you.
We stand hopeless, an empty shell without you.
You are our life, you are our hope, our destiny.
Our very breath.

Everything we have, or hoped for, belongs to you.
The whole world and its contents belong to you.
You are Master of it all.

So, Lord where is all this leading to?
Man is working aimlessly.
Thinking he is a winner,
Wanting to climb the highest peak.

But his true wealth is not in the earth.
Nothing he has can save him.
His search is in vain, his works are hopeless.
His life is snuffed out.

Let man therefore turn,
Turn and look, to see,
To listen, to hear your voice,
And reach for the prize, priceless
Everlasting riches, everlasting peace.
Everlasting glory, everlasting love.
In your presence, he will be.

THE BEAUTIFUL JOURNEY

The journey has begun,
It's a beautiful way, governed by His laws and truths.
And you will be led, as you can see
The road has two lanes

So, if you live in a castle,
or under a tree, and ate the fatted calf,
Instead of the lean and bony one,
If you sleep on a bed of velvet
And sweet-smelling roses,
Instead of the miry clay and dirt,
Whatever was your lot.
At the end of it all, it no longer gratifies the soul.

Today if you dine with me
Or refused my bread, if you make merry,
Or refused my song
Or you sit in a barrier of darkness,
Refusing the sunshine,
Whatever you choose, it's all in vain,
And counts for nothing in the end.

So, whatever was your lot or whatever you choose,
Only, let it lead you to the place in His presence.
For only once you will cross this path.
So, think not of the rich,
That he is better than the poor,
His glory will soon be gone,
And all will share a common place of abode.

Hence make preparation and stand your ground.
Take only what you need to go.
The armor to make it through the way,
The shield of faith,
And breastplate of righteousness,
The crown of salvation and belt of truth.
The sword of the spirit, His word.
With shoes of peace, the good news.
Praying at all times,
With praises and thanksgiving.

VESSELS OF HONOUR

We are made in His image and likeness
Vessels of honor for His glory.
The blueprint of the Master's touch

Like broken vessels we become vessels
of dishonor and pride,
Hate and hopelessness.
In pieces we fall.
But like a puzzle, He puts the pieces in place.
What appears crooked.

Beginning with no end,
The mountains rise higher and higher with no recourse.
But suddenly, He sweeps the stubbles away,
And behold vessels of honor arise again,
To resound His mighty works.

Who can stand in His way?
His love overshadows our faults.
Mercy and longsuffering abound.

So, stand up and entrust your frailty in His care.
The one who created each of us.
To be His vessels of honor and love.

YOU CAN NEVER STOP

You can never stop using the tools I gave you.
So, build your house strong,
Unshaken by the raging storms.

You can never go below.
Raise your eyebrows to the hills
and look above,
For there comes your salvation.

The Lord is my name.

You can never stop praying for that loved one,
For that neighbor or that friend.
Your hope is in the everlasting word,
Savior of the world, author of Life.

Yes, you can never stop believing,
For the just will live by faith,
And doubts will flee to nought.
So, stand still and persevere.

But today you must stop
And mesmerize your soul in my love
And see beyond the ashes,
Into this your new dimension,
For I am here
And I am unstoppable.

THE VAIN LIFE

Man! meaningless is your life.
Searching, looking, going in the wrong direction.
Woman you too, all riches and glamour is not the way.

This is the world then and now.
For I was clutched from the jaws of hell so I can tell.
It's not what you see or hear.
It's more than that.
It's not how you look, what you have, or what you can do.
It's more than that.

Each day unfolds into a new one
A step closer to all eternity.
Can you tell the day?

Did He not say "no man knows" the day?
Not even the angels,
He did say "watch and pray",
Do not be dismayed.
So, think again,
And do not lose your mind.
For life is indeed fragile
Handle with prayers.

AWAKE O SOUL

Nations of the world
Arise and look
What do you see?
What do you hear?

Beyond your imagination
And your understanding
Unfolds this great catastrophe.

Souls are plunged into death:
One thousand to the left
Ten thousand to the right
People are crying everywhere
Children deserted, with no one to care.

Disaster and lamentation
Fill the earth
Uncomforted souls are gone.

Nations of the earth,
God's chosen people,
What are you looking for?
Surely not a reed shaking in the wind
Or a rainbow in the clouds,
Is it a sign or a wonder you seek?

Stop and think, you have the mind of Christ.
These are the times foretold to you.
Anguish, torment, pain.
Pestilences in divers' places and grief.
Then why do you trade, your soul to the world?
Yes, it's not so simple as you thought.
And it's not as difficult as it sounds.
It's not business as usual.
Neither is it a complicated way.
For He is the way, light in the dark.

People of God, people of the world.
You ask over and over, which way to turn?
Is it to the right? Or is it to the left?
You know the answer.
But still, you linger on and say it will be soon.

Oh, foolish man,
Time is not yours to hold
You cannot create a single day.
You have wasted it all,
In vanity and pride,
In selfishness and greed,
With no power over death or life.
Your days are numbered.

As it is by the minutes, they flee by.
Grasp now this moment at hand and go to the plough,
With steadfast hands.
Never wavering, never looking back.
But with a clutch on His hem.
Never losing, never letting go!

TIME IS SHORT

Time is short,
It cannot be timed,
It cannot be measured with the hands of a clock.
It's rolling away, like the clouds,
And disappears into the unknown.

Who can bring it back again?
Who can stand it still for a second?
As one slumbers, He never sleeps.
And a new day is dawned.
In place of the one before.

Time is short.
From sunrise to sunset
We have no grasp.
We are all led like sheep to the pasture.
With compulsion we are led
And we acknowledge the hour,
Knowing it's the clock we cannot stop.

So, we clamor on and on
On borrowed time from the Lord.
And now, we must put on our boots of compassion,
And our coats of love,
To lighten the path for others.

Then, embrace it with passion.
Use it with diligence,
Enduring to the end
When time becomes timeless.
Today you must live your time.

LOVE SUPERCEDES

I am nothing if I have not loved.
And if I have not loved,
My faith is lost.
Sinking sand is all around,
So, stand firm.
For He is present all the way.
On solid ground we stand with Him.

Consider His words.
They are right and crystal clear,
A way, He did carve that we can go.

So, as you stand on the precipice at the edge of time,
Endow your feet and stand in love.
For worthy is the cause,
Making no room for your adversary.
So live, hope, have joy and faith.
But above all else, carry love,
For this is greater than the rest.
An everlasting gift from the heart of God Our Father.
Love each other.

WE WORSHIP YAHWEH

Praise and worship, love, and honor
Is what you seek oh Lord.
So, we bow to you, the everlasting rock,
On which we lean.

Day by day
The sun shines forth its glory.
The trees bow before you,
Swaying gently in reverence.
The waves usher in their mark of energy,
Greeting each other, as in relay.

As nature works in harmony,
The bees, the birds, and fishes
Never cease from their line of duty.
The seas and underworld
Stand still at your command.

But man, your treasured creation
Seems not to know his purpose.
He forgets his creator,
To whom honor is due,
And clings to every dark corner
And tries to hide his face from you,
Departing in his own ways.

So, Lord, in all this Dominion,
Too vast it is,
Let man stand up
And pay you homage, giving thanks always.
Let his praises ring out for ever.

THE ANCHOR OF HOPE

When all is closing in,
You cannot stretch your arms
Beyond the wall.
You cannot see beyond the borders,
Clouds of darkness hide your view.

Know there is One, who stretches
His arms to meet you where you are.
You are never hidden,
In the seas or beneath the earth.
In the valleys or mountain tops,
When all is going up and down,
In and out, backwards, and forward
With no clear direction,
Know for sure, He is the way.
The vision, and the light.
When life becomes uncertain
The storms are raging all around.
Lift up your eyes and know for sure,
He is the anchor you can hold.
When all have failed you, people, and
systems and whatsoever,
He cannot fail to His word,
As He promised, to always be with you.

When your heart is broken, and you feel much pain,
and despair beyond your capacity to hold.
Remember He mends the brokenhearted.
He is sailing the ship, with the broken mast.
Look to Him for He is the One.
Closer than a brother can be.
As He leads the rocky paths.
Have faith and assurance.
Thrusting thyself under His wings.

REDEEMED

You hide away my sins and shame,
and blot them out, as far as the east is from the West.
You cast them out and say I am free.
You call me a friend, never abandoned, never forsaken.
You cause me to abide in green pastures,
And my cup overflows, with goodness and mercy.
As I hear the whisper
Of the gentle breeze,
I can feel your presence.
My tears you wipe away, and springs
of joy has filled my heart.

Sorrows flee and laughter came,
Like fresh dew falling from above.
The powers of hell and darkness flee,
No longer have their grip on me.

I am amazed, bewildered,
Redeemed and free.
I do not deserve it.
So, I gave you praise and honor.
And I know you will receive it.

HIS PRESENCE

I lift up my eyes.
I cannot see beyond the clear blue skies,
But I know and feel your presence all around.
It's like a rippling wave that never ceases.
Like the sun that puts out its light,
Ever shining so brilliantly.
It's renewed day after day for all eternity.

And like a gentle breeze you keep saying
"I am here", and "you are in the palm of my hands."

How blessed I am that love has cast out all my fears,
as I strove forward,
Gliding over the dark clouds of life.
Inhaling the fresh aroma of your love.

With you as my magnet,
I will gather the wealth of your goodness,
And scatter the forbidden ones.

I will trust into your arms,
For you are my fortress
And I am your chosen gem.
Kept safe from all your enemies.

I will worship at thy holy mount,
For you are my banner, my warrior,
My King of peace,
And to you,
Heaven and earth will bow.
As they cannot deny the reason why!!

LIVE FOREVER

With clubs and swords, they came.
With a kiss, the arrest was quick.
The cries grew louder and louder,
Their minds, too dark to reason.
Their judgement was merely, of human instincts,
So, treason sounds like a reason.

Nonetheless they followed the path ahead.
Some out of revenge,
Some out of incitement,
Yet others out of mere curiosity.
Some in pain and sorrows,
Yet others, in a state of disbelief and mockery.
But all in all
As hope seemed hopeless
He chose no defense,
As we meant more than his life,
For by dying, we will live.

Condemned to die,
His cross overburdened but stood in glory.
His pain immense,
As He bore my sins, yours, and sins of the world.
Yet not the will of man,
But of God who sent Him.

For worthy is the sacrifice, for the lamb to bear.
Every second counted,
Every nail driven in,
Every drop of blood shed,
Was for you and for me,
So, he prayed forgiveness,
And hung alone, Knowing He did not want to lose us.

So, the earth refused Him,
An outburst of powers, as it trembles.
Victory over death,
Over the dark powers,
Over the master of lies and deceit.

He arose in shimmering dazzling raiment.
Death conquered,
We will live forever.
It's real!!! Declared the angels
He is not here, He is risen!!!

Happy resurrection day.

STAND FREE, ACQUITTED!

Are you ready?
Well then, get ready!!
The book will be opened.
What will be your defense?
No debate can substantiate your excuse.
What will be your choice of words?
For you have denied His word.

You are not to remain blinded,
And lack of understanding.
For you will stand before
The Judge of all judges.
With so much love in His heart.
You will depart in pain and sorrow.
For no iniquity can He bypass.

But right now, stand free
Of the cases separating you from Him.
You need to know, you are chosen,
That He made a way for you.
A master minded, victorious plan.
A shot from glory.
Before the foundations of the world.

Today you are your judge,
The choice will always be yours.
Your rights, He will not take.
So, try to understand your privileges.
Your breadth, Your choice, His love. His grace.
And set your house in order.

Pay heed to the voice, the One calling to you.
As life is short, a vapor.
Here now, disappears with a blink.
Set your mind on Him.
Higher let your goals be.
Run from disobedience and wickedness,
The enemies, who seek your soul.
Stand acquitted,
In His love forever,
When the book is opened.

UNENDING MERCY

You stand taller, than the highest peak.
You are more majestic than any other,
Forever the same.
You are set as flint,
And do not change.
Stern and upright judge you are.
Your heart of love has never tarnished.
Wisdom and righteousness sit with you,
And your mercy is undone.

Your path is clear,
Alight by your glory,
Amidst thorns and briers, you walked,
Cutting stones lie flat,
Their position commanded
By your graceful shadow.

You see through every dense, invisible cloud.
You need not the eyes of the blind,
For you give the sight.

You are a patient King
And do not judge your subjects
As you should.
One day stands as a year.
And this is why,
Man is spared this long.

How long will you wait for man?
Instead, you keep turning the pages
One more time,
One more chance
For you call man, your friend.

Reckoning stands in your dominion,
For righteousness inhabits your courts,
On bended knees.
Heaven and earth will bow, before thee,
The eternal King of glory.

THE GREAT "I AM"

You are ever present.
Even when I neglect to pay you honor,
Or lean on my failing strength,
Your spirit reminds me, day, and night,
In the dawning of the day,
Or in the sunset of the evening.
Even if it's raining or shining.
Your presence never leaves.

In all the seasons of the year,
Springtime and winter, autumn and summer,
Every grain of sand, every fallen leaf,
You know their numbers.
Endless throughout the ages.

Who will acknowledge these vast details?
And write their numbers,
from the ends of the earth?
For you do not need to calculate,
And do not stand misguided.

Great and sovereign creator, you are
Infinite and all knowing,
Even when, a report denotes gloom and despair.
You will say "not so",
"Look to me and declare your case,
For I have the last say".

You will always stand supreme.
The learned and the proud, their wisdom,
comparable to foolishness
And calamity their inheritance.
Uncertain are their ways.
But you Lord
Is the mighty One!
The everlasting God!
You are the great I Am.

HE IS EXALTED

To the one who owns it all.
The universe, the planets,
The heavens and the earth.
The one who never sleeps day or night.
It's all the same, His glory alights it all.

No one can dethrone Him
No one can exalt himself higher.
For He will always be,
Forever the same, Alpha and Omega.

To the mighty God who is just,
Full of love, for love is His name,
Healer of all diseases,
Comforter of the grief-stricken souls.
To this magnificent God
We Bow.

Send your glory Lord,
Send your peace in the midst of desolation.
Let the scoffers stop.
Let the unbeliever be confounded.
Let the haters bow in shame.
But let the meek see your face.
For these are the chosen few.

Let your powers be such,
That the skeptics and agnostics cannot explain.
But the just will know it's you.
For by faith, they walk.
They are not taken by surprise,
So, help them Lord,
To endure,
To Persevere,
To stand upright
And carry your banner all the way.

Printed in the United States
by Baker & Taylor Publisher Services